She Persisted

MARIAN ANDERSON

—INSPIRED BY—
She Persisted
by Chelsea Clinton & Alexandra Boiger

MARIAN ANDERSON

Written by
Katheryn Russell-Brown

Interior illustrations by
Gillian Flint

PHILOMEL

PHILOMEL BOOKS
An imprint of Penguin Random House LLC, New York

First published in the United States of America by Philomel Books,
an imprint of Penguin Random House LLC, 2022

Text copyright © 2022 by Chelsea Clinton
Illustrations copyright © 2022 by Alexandra Boiger

Penguin supports copyright. Copyright fuels creativity, encourages diverse
voices, promotes free speech, and creates a vibrant culture. Thank you for
buying an authorized edition of this book and for complying with copyright
laws by not reproducing, scanning, or distributing any part of it in any form
without permission. You are supporting writers and allowing Penguin to
continue to publish books for every reader.

Philomel Books is a registered trademark of Penguin Random House LLC.

Visit us online at penguinrandomhouse.com.

Library of Congress Cataloging-in-Publication Data is available.

Printed in the United States of America

HC ISBN 9780593403761
10 9 8 7 6 5 4 3 2 1
PB ISBN 9780593403785
10 9 8 7 6 5 4 3 2 1

WOR

Edited by Jill Santopolo and Talia Benamy.
Design by Ellice M. Lee.
Text set in LTC Kennerley.

The publisher does not have any control over and does not assume any
responsibility for author or third-party websites or their content.

☞ To the memory of ☜
my great-grandmother, Fanny Daniel Speese
(1872–1951), a woman of quiet and firm dignity,
and my grandmothers, Paulene Speese Jones
(1912–1994) and Katie King Russell (1914–1946).
All three believed strongly in education and justice.
Each of them persisted and thrived despite the
often hostile world they had to navigate.
—KRB

She Persisted

She Persisted: MARIAN ANDERSON

She Persisted: VIRGINIA APGAR

She Persisted: NELLIE BLY

She Persisted: RUBY BRIDGES

She Persisted: CLAUDETTE COLVIN

She Persisted: ROSALIND FRANKLIN

She Persisted: TEMPLE GRANDIN

She Persisted: FLORENCE GRIFFITH JOYNER

She Persisted: HELEN KELLER

She Persisted: CORETTA SCOTT KING

She Persisted: CLARA LEMLICH

She Persisted: MAYA LIN

She Persisted: WANGARI MAATHAI

She Persisted: WILMA MANKILLER

She Persisted: PATSY MINK

She Persisted: SALLY RIDE

She Persisted: MARGARET CHASE SMITH

She Persisted: SONIA SOTOMAYOR

She Persisted: MARIA TALLCHIEF

She Persisted: DIANA TAURASI

She Persisted: HARRIET TUBMAN

She Persisted: OPRAH WINFREY

She Persisted: MALALA YOUSAFZAI

Dear Reader,

As Sally Ride and Marian Wright Edelman both powerfully said, "You can't be what you can't see." When Sally said that, she meant that it was hard to dream of being an astronaut, like she was, or a doctor or an athlete or anything at all if you didn't see someone like you who already had lived that dream. She especially was talking about seeing women in jobs that historically were held by men.

I wrote the first *She Persisted* and the books that came after it because I wanted young girls—and children of all genders—to see women who worked hard to live their dreams. And I wanted all of us to see examples of persistence in the face of different challenges to help inspire us in our own lives.

I'm so thrilled now to partner with a sisterhood of writers to bring longer, more in-depth versions of these stories of women's persistence and achievement to readers. I hope you enjoy these chapter books as much as I do and find them inspiring and empowering.

And remember: If anyone ever tells you no, if anyone ever says your voice isn't important or your dreams are too big, remember these women. They persisted and so should you.

Warmly,

Chelsea Clinton

MARIAN ANDERSON

TABLE OF CONTENTS

Chapter 1: *A Community of Music* 1

Chapter 2: *Finishing School* 9

Chapter 3: *World Travels* 17

Chapter 4: *Marian Sings* 25

Chapter 5: *New Experiences* 34

Chapter 6: *Growing Legacies* 43

How You Can Persist 50

References 54

CHAPTER 1

A Community of Music

A long, long time ago, it was common for some mothers to deliver their babies at home. On February 27, 1897, Marian Elina-Blanche Anderson was born in a room in a house on Webster St. in South Philadelphia. Marian was Anna and John Anderson's first child. Then came Alyse, and next was Ethel.

Marian's parents worked hard to keep a roof over their heads. John worked in the refrigerator room at the Reading Terminal Market. He also sold ice and coal. Besides taking care of her three girls, Anna was a seamstress and she did other folks' laundry. Marian always looked forward to her dad coming home from work—especially on those Fridays when he brought pound cake!

Early on, Marian showed an interest in music. Before she turned two, she would sit at her toy piano, hit the keys, and make up songs. She loved hearing and making sounds with or without an instrument. Anna said Marian could stay busy for an hour clapping her hands, stomping her feet, and singing—*lala-lala-la*! Marian was delighted with all the different sounds she could make.

Marian couldn't help but love music. It was everywhere. At home, Anna and John sang hymns around the house, and the family sang songs together after dinner. After Marian's daddy bought a used piano, she would sit next to him on the bench and practice the scales. Sometimes he let Marian think she was teaching him how to play.

Just going outside was a musical adventure. One day when she was about eight years old, Marian went on an errand for her mother and heard a piano playing. She followed the sounds of the tinkling melody up some steps, and there she saw a woman in the window, hands on the piano keys, making beautiful music. The woman was brown, like Marian. *Hmmm*, Marian thought, *If she can, I can.*

Music was at school, too—in music class. And when other students had their music lessons in a nearby classroom, she could hear them singing through the walls. She was mesmerized. The sound of their voices was a sweet inspiration for young Marian, who sang along quietly. When she heard the singing, Marian no longer heard what her teacher was saying.

Music embraced Marian like a cozy blanket on a chilly night.

At age six, she joined the junior choir at Union Baptist Church. Marian's powerful voice stood out among the others. At age seven, the choir director had her sing a duet with another girl in the choir. Their song was "Dear to the Heart of the Shepherd." Marian practiced like she was going to sing at Carnegie Hall, one of the most famous concert halls in the country! The performance was a success. Everyone could hear the talent in Marian's voice. That was the first time that Marian Anderson sang in public.

Marian also sang duets with her aunt at church. Pretty soon her aunt was signing her up to sing at community events all around town. Marian was paid a quarter, sometimes fifty cents to sing.

That was a lot of money for a young person to earn back then. Marian became so popular, flyers were made to advertise her upcoming performances. One included her photograph and said, COME AND HEAR THE BABY CONTRALTO, TEN YEARS OLD!

Contralto is considered the lowest singing voice for a woman. Marian's voice was deep and

rich. But that wasn't all. One minute she could make her voice climb the scales higher and higher. The next, she could just as beautifully make her voice climb back down the scales. Her voice was like a bird in flight—it could fly up high *and* swoop down low. When Marian performed, the audience was in awe of her voice—an earful of stunning sounds.

In 1909, the year Marian turned twelve, her family experienced a devastating blow. One day at work, Marian's father had a horrible accident. He didn't get any better and died after Christmas. Marian kept a special place in her heart for him and held tight to all the happy memories. Sadly, the family didn't have any photographs of Daddy.

"Tragedy," Marian said later on, "had moved into our home."

Marian's family moved in with Daddy's parents and other family members. Sometimes as many as a dozen people lived in the small house. Daddy was gone, but Marian's family had lots of love and support from their church and their South Philadelphia community.

CHAPTER 2

Finishing School

When it was time to start high school, Marian couldn't go. Her family didn't have enough money to pay for schoolbooks, clothes, or activities. They also needed Marian to work so she could help with the bills. To make money, Marian cleaned other people's houses and took singing jobs. By this time, she could earn five dollars for performing at an event. Whenever Marian got paid, she gave two dollars to her mother, a dollar each to Alyse and Ethel, and kept a dollar for herself.

As more and more people heard her voice, she was invited to participate in different programs around town. After hearing Marian sing at Union Baptist, Roland Hayes, a famous classical singer, said she had a special gift. He told Marian that with professional training, her voice would sound even more incredible. Marian yearned to attend music school, but there was no money for that.

The members of Union Baptist were proud of Marian. She was their community jewel. They raised money to pay for Marian's music lessons and hoped that one day the world would hear her voice. With their gift, Marian went to enroll at the Philadelphia Music Academy. When she arrived, she sat down in the room with other young ladies. She waited hours for her turn. Marian was the only Black girl in the room and the last person who was called. When she asked for an application, the young woman told her, "We don't take colored."

Marian couldn't believe her ears. She went straight home and told her mother what happened. Anna assured Marian that there would be some other way for her to get music training.

Even though Jim Crow, the rules that made life unequal for Black citizens, had long been present, the music school's rejection was a painful punch to Marian's heart. They hadn't heard her sing. They hadn't given her a chance.

Growing up, she knew about segregation laws that allowed Whites to treat Black people like second-rate citizens. Some stores only served Black customers after they helped White customers. Some parts of the city were off-limits to Black residents. "Sometimes the trolley cars would pass you by and not pick you up," Marian remembered.

Marian couldn't get into music school, but nothing could stop her from taking music lessons. She persisted until she found a singing teacher. Mary Saunders Patterson, her first instructor, was a soprano singer who lived in the neighborhood. Mrs. Patterson taught fifteen-year-old Marian how to project her voice to the ceiling.

When Marian started performing in different cities, she had more encounters with segregation. At age seventeen, she took her first trip to the Deep South. When she and her mother changed trains at the Washington, DC, station, Marian noticed that

the waiting room for Whites was much nicer than the one for Black travelers. On the train, all the Black riders had to sit in the front car of the train. It was smelly, hot, and dirty. The unfair treatment made Marian feel ashamed, even though she hadn't done anything wrong.

At age eighteen, Marian was finally able to start high school. The People's Chorus, a local singing group that Marian belonged to, raised money so she could enroll at William Penn High School. Marian was glad she could attend high school, but she had a tough time. She struggled through typing, bookkeeping, and shorthand classes. Those subjects didn't hold Marian's interest—she was bored.

During a visit to Wilmington, Delaware, Marian met a young man named Orpheus Hodge Fisher. He was also in high school and was studying to be an architect. His skin was very pale, so even though he was Black, some people thought he was White. Orpheus, whose nickname was King, began dating Marian and was a regular visitor at her family's home. King often brought along a borrowed phonograph, which was sort of like a record player, so they could listen to music.

After they dated for a short while, King

proposed marriage. Marian loved King, but she told him no. She knew that getting married would end her singing career. Even with all the challenges she faced, what Marian wanted most was to sing.

Marian attended William Penn High for three years and later transferred to the South Philadelphia High School for Girls. In 1921, when she was twenty-four years old, she graduated. Although Marian completed high school later than many of her peers, what matters most is that she finished. She did what she set out to do.

CHAPTER 3

World Travels

Marian didn't become famous overnight. She had downs with the ups. After high school, she continued taking singing lessons with Giuseppe Boghetti, a well-regarded opera teacher. While working with him, she learned songs by English, German, and Italian composers. Church members from Union Baptist supported Marian again and paid for her music sessions.

In 1924, Marian was scheduled to give a

recital at New York's Town Hall. After weeks of preparation, it was time for the performance. She had been told there would be a large crowd. Marian got a rude surprise. When she went onstage, she could see that more than half of the seats were empty. Even worse, the newspapers wrote negative reviews. Some critics said her singing wasn't so great.

Marian was embarrassed. She told Giuseppe that she would never sing in public again. "The dream," Marian said, "was over."

She continued to work on her singing in private. After several months, Marian dusted away her doubts and entered a competition held by the New York Philharmonic orchestra. She won! They picked her as the best singer out of the three hundred contestants. Her prize was to perform

with the orchestra in front of an audience of more than 7,500 people. Marian put on a show! This time the critics were bowled over.

After the performance, Marian was in high demand. She and Billy King, her talented pianist, traveled by train to perform at Black colleges across the South. Marian had come a long way from the fifty cents she earned for singing songs as a little girl. By this time, she could make $350 for one performance—that was enough money to buy a car! Things were going so well that Marian could help her family pay bills. Marian was happy to call Wanamaker's department store and tell them that her mother would no longer be cleaning and scrubbing their floors. Her mother, she announced, "will not be coming back to work."

Although there were more opportunities for Marian to sing, she was performing at the same places, in front of the same audiences. Rarely was she invited to perform in an opera. The hum of Jim Crow was still there. Marian knew that America had put a ceiling on her talent and that would limit how high she could rise.

Once again, Marian decided to bet on herself. She chose to leave the United States and move to Europe. She believed that a world stage would find room for her voice.

In 1927, when she boarded an ocean liner for England, she joined a long line of Black artists who'd left America to find better treatment in

other countries. Josephine Baker, Paul Robeson, James Baldwin, and her mentor Roland Hayes had all moved to Europe. After she saved enough money, Marian was ready to go. Bon voyage!

For over a decade, Marian spent most of her time touring across Europe. She started in England and sang from one place to the next—in Scandinavia, France, Germany, Finland, and the Soviet Union. It took a lot of effort to learn to sing songs that were written in other languages. Marian decided to learn to speak French and German to make sure she understood the words she was singing.

The international audiences were open-minded and curious. They showed Marian great respect. In some places she was treated like royalty. Scandinavia had "Marian mania"! People packed the halls to hear Marian's three-octave voice singing opera, folk songs, and African American spirituals. She was in high demand. In one year, Marian gave more than a hundred concerts.

When she performed in Austria, the famous conductor Arturo Toscanini attended her recital. After hearing Marian sing, he visited her backstage. He told her that a voice so magnificent only comes along once in a century. Marian was flattered but she was too nervous to get her words out. Newspapers everywhere published stories about the conductor's high praise for Marian.

No matter where she was in the world, King knew how to find Marian. He wrote letters to her and begged her to write back to him. Marian cared about King, but she was busy and didn't usually take time to send him letters. King still wanted

Marian to be his wife but decided he had waited long enough. Even though she had turned him down, Marian was heartbroken when she found out that King had married another woman.

CHAPTER 4
....

Marian Sings

By the time Marian returned home to America, she had become an international singing sensation. She had performed for kings and queens and presidents of other countries. Unfortunately, in the United States, the laws still allowed people to treat others differently based on their skin color.

In 1936, Marian received an extraordinary invitation. President Franklin Roosevelt and First Lady Eleanor Roosevelt asked her to visit the

White House. Marian was the first Black artist to perform at the president's house. After the visit, the first lady and Marian became fast friends. Both women believed in civil rights for all people. Both knew it was wrong for laws to discriminate against Black people. Their special bond had an impact on civil rights that no one could have imagined.

The following year, Marian sang before an

all-White audience at Princeton University. After her performance was over, there was a problem. The local hotel did not allow Black people. Tired Marian had no place to lay her head. When famous scientist Albert Einstein, a professor at the university, heard about this, he welcomed Marian into his home. Albert, who had been discriminated against because he was Jewish, knew it was wrong.

In 1939, Howard University's School of Music asked Marian to give a concert. She had performed there several times before and agreed to another visit. This time, however, because Marian was so popular, they needed to find a larger place to have the concert. They asked to use Constitution Hall, Washington, DC's, largest auditorium. It was a beautiful theater and could hold four thousand people.

"No" was the answer. The Daughters of the American Revolution, the group in charge of Constitution Hall, said Black people were not allowed to perform in the building. When she heard about this, Marian said, "I am shocked beyond words to be barred from the capital of my own country." Marian wasn't alone. Lots of people were upset that the organization refused to let her sing. The Daughters of the American Revolution refused to change their decision. They took a special vote and agreed to keep their unfair, prejudiced rules.

There was a big scramble to find a place where Marian could perform. Both Walter White and Charles Houston, who worked with the National Association for the Advancement of Colored People, a civil rights group, met with other people to figure out how to solve the problem. Also, a community group was quickly formed to support Marian. The Marian Anderson Citizens Committee searched for places where the concert could be held.

The first lady believed that Marian was being treated unfairly, so she used her voice to support Marian's voice. After writing about the controversy in her newspaper column, the first lady wrote a letter to the president of the Daughters of the American Revolution and said she was canceling her membership.

Eleanor Roosevelt's actions were big news. People wrote letters, sent telegrams, and signed petitions supporting Marian. It made her feel good to have so many people on her side. Everywhere Marian went, people asked her about the

"Washington situation." She knew something big was brewing.

The recital was set for April 9, 1939, Easter Sunday. After lots of discussion and planning, there was talk about having the recital outdoors on the steps of the Lincoln Memorial. Marian wasn't sure this was a good idea. She was used to singing in concert halls and had never sung outside. She was worried about the weather, too—it might snow. After talking with her mother and thinking more about it, Marian agreed to give an outside concert.

Walter White, Charles Houston, and Eleanor Roosevelt faced another big challenge. They had to make sure there was a large crowd to welcome Marian.

On Easter Sunday, a sea of people showed up

to greet Marian. More than 75,000 people—adults and children of all races—braved the brisk weather to hear her astonishing voice. Millions more listened to the recital on the radio.

Marian looked regal as she was escorted onto the stage. She wore a bold orange silk blouse and black skirt, and a long brown mink coat. The huge crowd cheered loudly. Then it fell silent. Marian stood in front of the bank of microphones, closed her eyes, opened her mouth, and for twenty-five minutes, she sang. She began with "My Country, 'Tis of Thee" and ended with "My Soul's Been Anchored in the Lord." Marian's velvet-smooth voice was soul stirring. When she finished, she told the crowd, "I can't tell you what you have done for me today. I thank you from the bottom of my heart again and again."

That day, Marian showed the world what Jim Crow had tried to hide.

Nearly twenty-five years later, on those same steps, Dr. Martin Luther King Jr. gave his "I Have a Dream" speech. Marian's actions had blazed a trail for others to demand fair treatment.

CHAPTER 5

New Experiences

Marian's performance at the Lincoln Memorial had a big impact on her career. The support she received for her performance was a sign of progress for the civil rights movement. But even though Marian had stood up to the Daughters of the American Revolution and put on an unforgettable concert for thousands of people, Jim Crow was still the law in many places. The evening of her Easter concert, Marian had to stay overnight with friends, since many hotels in Washington, DC, didn't allow Black people.

The Lincoln Memorial concert did lead to some good opportunities for Marian. Now that her audiences were larger, she could tell more people about civil rights. Over the next few years, Marian grew even more accustomed to taking trips around the world. As a US Goodwill Ambassador, she performed in India, Japan, Thailand, and the Caribbean. Marian packed heavy for her trips. She made sure to take everything she needed. Sometimes she had as many as twenty bags! She carried clothes, purses, hats, shoes, concert gowns, and gloves. She also packed dishes, towels, a sleeping bag, a sewing machine, and a hot plate. She also liked to take her records.

Marian learned that no matter what she

packed, each trip was a unique experience. On a visit to Brazil, she had a strange encounter. During intermission she returned to her dressing room. Her assistant told her that a doctor and another man were there to see her. The men were speaking in Portuguese, a language Marian didn't know. It took a few minutes before she understood that they wanted to examine her throat! Marian wasn't sure what to do. Was this something they did in some countries? She didn't want to be rude, since she had to get back onstage, so she agreed to their request.

The doctor looked down her throat. The other man did the same. The two men spoke excitedly to one another. Then they quickly shook hands with Marian and left. Perhaps the men had been shocked to hear her sing such extraordinarily high and low notes and wanted to see if she had a normal-looking throat. Marian never found out who the men were or why they wanted to examine her throat!

Three years after Marian sang on the steps of the Lincoln Memorial, she received an unexpected invitation. The Daughters of the American Revolution wanted her to perform at Constitution Hall. She decided to accept their offer since the United States was fighting in World War II and the concert would raise money for the war effort. But before Marian said yes, she had one demand: no segregated seating. They agreed, and nearly half of the people who attended the 1943 concert were Black.

There was another surprise a few months later. King and Marian had stayed in touch over the years. After King's first marriage ended, they started dating again. King once again wanted to settle down with Marian. And finally, Marian was ready to settle down with King. In 1943, nearly thirty years after they first met, Marian and King got married. They had a small private ceremony in Bethel, Connecticut. Marian said that marrying King was "worth waiting for."

The couple wanted to live in a house that wasn't too far from New York City, so Marian could attend events and see her family. King was excited to start looking for a home. But finding a house to buy was easier said than done. Each time they picked a house, something went wrong. Sometimes the sellers didn't realize that King was Black. And when they found out that his wife was Marian Anderson, who was by then a well-known

Black classical singer, the negotiations ended. It didn't matter that she was one of the most famous singers in the world. Houses he had looked at were suddenly no longer available.

It took King more than a year and many, many trips all over New York, Connecticut, and New Hampshire to find an old farmhouse, in Danbury, Connecticut, that they could buy. It was an hour and a half drive from New York. The house needed lots of repairs. But King was an architect, so he knew what to fix and how to fix it. They named their farmhouse "Marianna"—a combination of Marian and Anna, her mother's name.

Marian had accomplished her career goals. She was recognized around the world, had performed on several continents, sung on famous stages, mastered songs in different languages, and had millions of fans. But she was rarely asked to perform in an opera on the American stage. Marian had always loved opera. She was captivated by the stories and the dramatic singing. So in 1955, when

she was invited to perform with the New York Metropolitan Opera, it was a thrilling surprise. She joined the cast of *A Masked Ball*, and played the part of Ulrica, a fortune-teller. Performing at the Met was a dream come true for Marian. The audience showed how excited they were to hear her voice. They clapped loudly, chanted her name, and gave her a standing ovation. Some people shed tears of joy. Marian's mom beamed with pride as she watched her sing.

CHAPTER 6

Growing Legacies

The year 1964 did not begin on a happy note. On January 10, Marian's mother died. She was eighty-nine years old. Marian tried to avoid being sad by staying busy with work. Her mother had always been there to encourage her and to help her make important decisions.

Before her mother died, Marian had already started making plans to retire. She was ready to step off the stage after performing for sixty years.

By the end of her career, she had more than seventy music recordings. Marian planned a farewell tour to say thank you to her fans in fifty cities across the country. Constitution Hall was the first stop, and Carnegie Hall was the place she gave her final recital. Fans bought tickets to hear Marian's incredible contralto onstage one last time.

Now that she had more time at home, Marian found new hobbies. She loved cooking and trying new recipes. She had a garden and especially loved watching her strawberries grow. She also enjoyed taking photographs and developing them in her darkroom. There was always something to do on the farm. They had dogs, sheep, cows, horses, pigs, and chickens.

Most evenings after dinner, King and Marian would take a walk. Then they'd sit in their favorite

chairs and watch television. Even though Marian didn't really like watching TV shows, she enjoyed relaxing at home with King.

After Marian retired, she received lots of big awards for being a musical genius. Dozens of colleges awarded her special diplomas. She also visited

universities and music schools to talk with students about her legendary career.

Early in her career, Marian had started a scholarship to support students interested in singing classical music. She wanted to help them develop their music skills and help them with the costs of vocal lessons. Over the years, hundreds of talented vocalists have been awarded Marian Anderson scholarships. Marian's voice also inspired a new generation of famous opera singers, including Jessye Norman, Kathleen Battle, and Denyce Graves.

In 1986, after a long illness, King died. As sad as it was, Marian and King had been fortunate. They had enjoyed over forty years of a happy marriage. And on April 8, 1993, seven years after King's passing, Marian died too. She was ninety-six years old. She had lived the last year of her life in Portland, Oregon, where she stayed with her nephew, music conductor James DePreist, and his wife. Marian didn't want to leave her Connecticut farmhouse, but for health reasons she wanted to be close to her family.

What a life Marian Anderson lived! Her life offers lessons for each one of us. Marian believed in herself. She worked hard. She strived to do her best. She wasn't afraid to try new things. And she didn't give up when she hit a roadblock.

Marian had the love and support of her South Philadelphia community. Donations from church members, neighbors, and friends had made it possible for Marian to take music lessons. And her community gave her something worth way more than money: an anchor. No matter what, she could always go home to the place that had lifted her up when she was a little girl and encouraged her undeniable talent. Their support and love helped Marian develop pride and self-confidence. So when the law said that people who looked like Marian were second-class citizens, she knew that wasn't true. She was just as good as anybody else.

Marian never forgot that South Philadelphia was where her love of music began and where her talent sprouted. The community she loved and the one that loved her back had made it possible for her to live out her dream. All Marian wanted, she said, was to "sing and share" with the whole world. And that's just what she did.

HOW YOU CAN PERSIST

by Katheryn Russell-Brown

Here are some activities you can do to celebrate Marian Anderson's life and musical legacy:

1. Learn to sing a song you like in another language.
2. Offer to help a family member or member of your community achieve a goal. You can do this in many different

ways. You can volunteer your time, be a good listener, or donate part of your allowance to someone in need.

3. Write out a list of some of the places that Marian traveled to, including the method of transportation she used. Write out a list of three places you would like to travel to and how you would get there.
4. Write a song about Marian and sing it to a friend, a family member, or a classmate.
5. Plant strawberries and watch them grow.
6. If you see that someone is being treated unfairly, do what you can to make the situation better. If it helps you to think about it, write a few sentences on what you could do to help.

Acknowledgments

It's hard to imagine a world without persisters! Let's celebrate them by being persisters, supporting persisters and sharing their stories.

References

BOOKS & ARTICLES

Anderson, Marian. *My Lord, What a Morning: An Autobiography*. Chicago: University of Illinois Press, 1956.

Ault, Alicia. "How Marian Anderson Became an Iconic Symbol for Equality," *Smithsonian Magazine*, August 14, 2019. smithsonianmag

.com/smithsonian-institution/how-marian
-anderson-became-iconic-symbol-equality
-180972898.

Black, Allida M. "Championing a Champion: Eleanor Roosevelt and the Marian Anderson 'Freedom Concert,'" *Presidential Studies Quarterly*, Fall 1990, Vol. 20(4): 719–736.

Freedman, Russell. *The Voice That Challenged a Nation: Marian Anderson and the Struggle for Equal Rights*. Boston: Houghton Mifflin Harcourt, 2004.

Jones, Victoria Garrett. *Marian Anderson: A Voice Uplifted*. New York: Sterling Press, 2008.

Keiler, Allan. *Marian Anderson: A Singer's Journey*. Chicago: University of Illinois, 2000.

National Public Radio. "Denied a Stage, She Sang for a Nation," April 9, 2014. npr.org/2014/04/09/298760473/denied-a-stage-she-sang-for-a-nation.

Ryan, Pam Muñoz, and Brian Selznick. *When Marian Sang: The True Recital of Marian Anderson*. New York: Scholastic Press, 2002.

WEBSITES & VIDEOS

American Experience: Voice of Freedom. pbs.org/video/voice-of-freedom-crx5pq

American Masters: *Marian Anderson: The Whole World in Her Hands.* pbs.org/wnet/americanmasters/this-historic-marian-anderson-performance-made-her-an-icon-of-the-civil-rights-movement/14241

National Marian Anderson Museum marianandersonhistoricalsociety.weebly.com/biography.html

KATHERYN RUSSELL-BROWN is a children's book author, professor of law, and director of the Race and Crime Center for Justice at the University of Florida. She is the author of many award-winning and critically acclaimed books, including *Little Melba and Her Big Trombone*, *A Voice Named Aretha*, and *She Was the First! The Trailblazing Life of Shirley Chisholm*, which won a 2021 NAACP Image Award. Upcoming projects include a picture book biography titled *Not Too Tired for Justice: Black Women and the Civil Rights Movement*. Katheryn was born in New York City and grew up in Oakland, California.

You can visit Katheryn online at
krbrown.net
and follow her on Twitter
@KRussellBrown

GILLIAN FLINT has worked as a professional illustrator since earning an animation and illustration degree in 2003. Her work has since been published in the UK, USA and Australia. In her spare time, Gillian enjoys reading, spending time with her family and puttering about in the garden on sunny days. She lives in the northwest of England.

Courtesy of the illustrator

You can visit Gillian Flint online at
gillianflint.com
or follow her on Twitter
@GillianFlint
and on Instagram
@gillianflint_illustration

CHELSEA CLINTON is the author of the #1 *New York Times* bestseller *She Persisted: 13 American Women Who Changed the World*; *She Persisted Around the World: 13 Women Who Changed History*; *She Persisted in Sports: American Olympians Who Changed the Game*; *Don't Let Them Disappear: 12 Endangered Species Across the Globe*; *It's Your World: Get Informed, Get Inspired & Get Going!*; *Start Now!: You Can Make a Difference*; with Hillary Clinton, *Grandma's Gardens* and *Gutsy Women*; and, with Devi Sridhar, *Governing Global Health: Who Runs the World and Why?* She is also the Vice Chair of the Clinton Foundation, where she works on many initiatives, including those that help empower the next generation of leaders. She lives in New York City with her husband, Marc, their children and their dog, Soren.

Courtesy of the author

You can follow Chelsea Clinton on Twitter
@ChelseaClinton
or on Facebook at
facebook.com/chelseaclinton

ALEXANDRA BOIGER has illustrated nearly twenty picture books, including the She Persisted books by Chelsea Clinton; the popular Tallulah series by Marilyn Singer; and the Max and Marla books, which she also wrote. Originally from Munich, Germany, she now lives outside of San Francisco, California, with her husband, Andrea, daughter, Vanessa, and two cats, Luiso and Winter.

Photo credit: Vanessa Blasich

You can visit Alexandra Boiger online at
alexandraboiger.com
or follow her on Instagram
@alexandra_boiger

Read about more inspiring women in the

She Persisted series!